I n true, Real Man fashion, this book offers food for thought.

Not to mention the fact that if you're ever stuck in France, it also offers a way to avoid starvation:

Take the book, place it in a 350-degree oven for 20 minutes and smother with ketchup.

Admittedly, a Real Man will not find this as satisfying as a cheeseburger.

But it's certainly more palatable than, say, quiche.

Real Men Don't Cook Quiche

The Real Man's Cookbook

Scott Redman
Edited by Bruce Feirstein

Illustrated by Lee Lorenz

PUBLISHED BY POCKET BOOKS NEW YORK

This essay is dedicated to David Redman.
A Real Man whose heart was as big
as his appetite.

* * *

All books are collaborative efforts. And since Real Men *do* give
credit where credit is due, the following people must be thanked
for their contributions: Marty Asher, Roger Bilheimer, Anne Mait-
land, Peter Minichiello, Trish Todd, Nina Jorgensen, Darlene De-
Lillo, and Milton Charles from Pocket Books; Jacques Chazaud;
Lee Lorenz (whose drawings are as important as any word in
this essay); the Irv Schecter Company; the Ziegler Diskant talent
agency; Nancy Jean Gell; Tim Bernett; Steve Cass; Jake Bloom;
Jonathan Roberts and, finally, three people who made everything
possible: Frank E. and Suzanne J. Schwartz, and Jim Morgan,
from *Playboy* magazine.

Scott Redman
Bruce Feirstein
September, 1982

Text Copyright © 1982 by Bruce Feirstein
Illustrations Copyright © 1982 by Pocket Books, a Simon and
Schuster Division of Gulf & Western Corporation

ISBN: 0-671-46308-X

First Pocket Books printing November, 1982

10 9 8 7 6 5 4 3 2 1

POCKET and colophon are registered trademarks of Simon &
Schuster

Printed in the U.S.A.

Design by Jacques Chazaud

Contents

1

Introduction

Flex Crush was sitting at the Formica counter of Rosie's all-night diner in Tenafly, New Jersey. The restaurant smelled of bacon, fresh-brewed coffee and No-Doz. The fluorescent lighting glared. It was 5:30 A.M., and dawn was about to break over what passes for a horizon in the Garden State.

As Flex used a poppy-seed roll to wipe up the remains of a half dozen fried eggs from his plate— noting that Real Men do not believe in cholesterol— he made his final pronouncement on food.

"Real Men don't cook," Flex sighed, "they thaw."

With this, the self-proclaimed Last Real Man in America stood, paid the check and walked out to drive his 18-wheel Kenworth onto the entrance ramp of the New Jersey State Turnpike, which many suspect is the final resting place of Jimmy Hoffa. Having consumed a full breakfast, Flex was ready to roll on another high-speed, cross-country, nuclear-waste delivery.

Yet as he pulled out of the parking lot, heading for the Vince Lombardi toll plaza, something he said struck us as odd.

Perhaps Flex—the divine arbiter of all things Real Man-ish, the great soothsayer and Kunta Kinte of American Real Men—well, perhaps Flex was wrong.

For while it is true there may be better places for a man to distinguish himself than the kitchen (including Sevilla bull-fighting arenas, the Falkland Islands, the Chicago Commodities exchange and center ice at a Rangers game), there is nevertheless no shame in his being able to find his way around a kitchen.

Especially if he's stuck in a logging camp during an avalanche, trying to woo Candice Bergen or just having friends over to break bread on the Real Man's high holy day—Superbowl Sunday—when no self-respecting Real Man restaurant owner would be open in the first place.

This book is designed to help men survive under these straits.

Because, after all, it only stands to reason that if a Real Man can put together the interstate-highway system, surely he ought to be able to put together a decent meal for his buddies.

2

An Overview of Food

In the beginning, everything lived in the sea. It was cold. And dark. And a little too heavily salted for most people's taste.

Lo and behold, one day things began to change.

A certain group of fish decided to leave. They were hungry. And thirsty. And, realizing that it was impossible to get a decent cup of coffee under water, they took to the land in search of a hot meal.

(Certain scientists have postulated this group of sea hunters were known as the "Lloyd Bridges school of fish," but this has yet to be scientifically proven.)*

Anyway, to make a long story short, this is how modern man came into being.

But we're not talking about Cro-Magnon man. Or Neanderthal man. No. The man we're talking about here is beef-eating man. A *Real Man* who would later invent the hamburger. And beer. And French fries. A Man who would reject such foolish notions as calories, nutrition and vitamins—and would understand that a well-balanced diet consists of a quarter-pounder in each hand.

---

*On another note, it's theorized that a separate school of fish existed which found life too hectic in prehistoric urban society and chose to return to the sea. These spineless, gutless mammals are known today as dolphins and whales, and their wimpy traits may account for their current status as the darlings of the quiche-eating environmentalist crowd.

If you don't believe this, just consider the personalities of leading TV animal stars: Rin Tin Tin was a Real Man; ditto for Trigger, Mister Ed and Lassie. But Flipper? We strongly suspect he lives in Marina Del Rey, drives a Corvette and munches on quiche at every opportunity.

The Evolution of the Real Man

And so it came to pass that the ritual of eating was established.

Fire, for example, was discovered because Real Men had a primeval instinct to barbecue.

The church immediately recognized the trend and incorporated the phrase "thou preparest a table before me" in their service.

And this, of course, is without taking into account such important cultural milestones as the Last Supper, Jack Nicholson ordering a chicken-salad sandwich in *Five Easy Pieces* or the Earl of Sandwich inventing convenience foods.

But we digress.

The point is that food has always played an integral part in the Real Man's life. Food is the thing that fuels Real Men on the professional bowling tour. It's the primary source of nourishment for Mafia hit men, corporate lawyers, steelworkers, and auto-repossession experts. Food gives Men something to do at half time; it's a pleasant diversion at family gatherings (enabling you to avoid discussing religion with your aunts), and, of course, without food there would be no wonderful Real Man expressions like "Eat my dust," "Bite the bullet," "I'm going to chew you up and spit you out," and the ever-popular "This ain't gonna be a piece of cake."

In addition to all this, we must not overlook the fact that—perhaps most importantly—eating is an essential part of the mating process.

First, because all Real Men know that a good meal will always impress a date.

And, second, because it will give them the strength and stamina to go the distance at the end of the evening.

Real Men, you see, recognize that they have more than one kind of insatiable appetite.

Real Man
Cooking Lesson #1

Q. How does a Real Man
blanch broccoli?

A. He screams at it.

An Interview
With the Ultimate
Real Man Chef

The problem was obvious.

Having firmly established that Real Men don't eat quiche, millions of people (thousands, anyway) have hungered after a simple answer:

Just what *do* Real Men eat?

What are the foodstuffs that satiate men like Nick Nolte, Chuck Norris, Ned Beatty, Paul Harvey or the Dallas Cowboys—when there's no McDonald's, Kentucky Fried Chicken or Trucker's 76 Pit Stop within excessive speeding distance?

Thirsting after this knowledge, we decided to visit the world's foremost expert in Real Men's cuisine, Rocco (the Knife) Tortellini, current head chef at Joliet State Prison.

As we began the interview, Rocco was putting the finishing touches on a luncheon for 1,200 close friends and former business associates.

Q. What are you serving today?

A. Twelve to 15 for grand theft, conspiracy and extortion, reducible to six weeks for good behavior.

Q. No. We meant for lunch.

A. Oh. It's something called prison stew. The recipe is 1,200 pounds of beef, plus 400 pounds of potatoes and a handful of vegetables. You cut it all up, throw it in a pot and let it simmer until parole.

Q. Does anybody complain about the food?

A. Not if they're smart.

Q. What do you think of the state of Real Men's cuisine today?

A. It makes me sick. In the old days, Real Men ate canned foods—and the can. They ate frozen foods frozen. They ate beef. Steak. Hamburgers, cheeseburgers, chili burgers, bacon burgers, pizza burgers and ribs. Anything they could kill with a gun or grill.* But today things are different. You got guys in here who want stuff like Brie. Perrier. Cold pasta salad. Poached salmon in dill. I can understand poaching diamonds. But salmon? Next thing, they'll probably want finger bowls on the tables. If they'd served that stuff in the old days, you woulda had guys breakin' out not for freedom, but a decent meal.

Q. Why do you think this has happened?

A. I suppose it has something to do with the element crime is attracting today. When I first started, you had thugs, button men, and racketeers. But now you've got guys in here for computer crime. Insurance fraud. Pansy stuff. I think the change started in the early '70s when we had all those guys from Watergate passing through. One of them sent back a piece of meat that was too tough. Now that's a wimp for you. In the old days, a Real Man prided himself on being able to chew through cement.

As Rocco continued preparing lunch, the inmates poured into the dining room. He was correct that times had changed; instead of being filled with "hard guys" like George Raft, Jimmy Cagney or Burt Lancaster (as the birdman of Alcatraz), the joint was rotten with cocaine dealers, income tax evaders and Billie Sol Estes-type financial swindlers. It looked more

---

*Actually, grilling was always the Real Man's favorite way to cook. After a tough day with the DA, it was nice to be on the other side of the table for a change.

It happens everytime the cook puts too much rosemary in the Veal Marengo.

like teatime in the IBM corporate dining room than chowtime at the Rock.

Glancing over the crowd, Rocco shrugged and continued cooking.

Q. Getting back to food, what are the basic eating habits of Real Men?

A. Real Men eat standing up. They eat with their friends. They eat with gusto. They also eat with veterans of foreign wars, cutthroat corporate executives and union officials.

Q. Is there anyone a Real Man won't eat with?

A. Hair stylists, distant cousins, interior decorators and anybody celebrating victory at a backgammon tournament.

Q. What's the main reason Real Men eat?

A. It cuts down on small talk.

Q. What about foreign food? Do Real Men eat guacamole? French food? Mexican food?

A. What do *you* think?

Q. Well, if you were stuck in a foreign country, there's a chance you might have to—

A. Wrong. When a Real Man gets hungry overseas, he eats K rations. Or he stops in the cafeteria of the American embassy and gets a real meal.

Q. Do Real Men always finish what's on their plates?

A. Yeah. But only because they're hungry. Never because children are starving in places like India, Europe, French restaurants or the Republic of Togo.

Q. Do you have any tips for Real Men chefs who might be reading this book?

A. Yeah. Always make sure your oven is hot enough to melt a Chevrolet.

Q. What about condiments?

A. I'm Catholic. I don't believe in birth control.

At this point, the interview was suddenly cut short; inside the dining room the inmates were pounding the table for dinner—and it was Rocco's duty to answer their chant of, "Granola, Granola, Granola."

Unfortunately, this was to be his last duty as chef.

In Rocco's own words, he'd "cooked his own goose" by serving one Real Man meal too many—and was savagely brutalized with cold pasta by several dozen irate inmates who were serving time for "grave offenses in bad taste" committed against the editors of *Architectural Digest*.

Yet Rocco will not be forgotten.

Many of his recipes are reproduced in this book; in the end, he died so that you can eat better.

Real Man Cooking Lesson #2: 5 things that taste better with Jack Daniels poured on them

1. Wheaties

2. Chicken

3. Ice

4. Salad

5. Any meal on an airplane

A Tour Through a Strange Place: The Kitchen

As we pointed out before, despite all myths to the contrary, Real Men can cook. They can prepare meals with style, panache and grace. (They can also prepare meals with fire, gas or napalm, but we're getting a bit ahead of ourselves here.)

The point is, however, that if a Real Man was trapped in the French embassy, he could probably flambée his way out. A Real Man can smell a bad cantaloupe at 35 yards (but would never embarrass his wife by doing so), and it only stands to reason that if the true definition of a Real Man is somebody who can put together an Indy 500 Offenhouser engine blindfolded, then surely a small breakfast should be no problem.

As with everything else, however, you have to take things one step at a time. (Alas, even a Real Man must learn to walk before he enters the decathlon.)

Thus we start with the kitchen.

For those of you who aren't intimately familiar with this turf, a kitchen is the area that most meals emanate from. (At least those that haven't been ordered in.) A kitchen is to cooking what France was to World War II: a horrible place to visit, but nevertheless someplace to do battle. (It's also something that adds considerably to the resale value of any house or condominium, and thus should not be removed or turned into a two-bay muffler shop.)

A Real Man's kitchen is a perfect reflection of the Real Man himself. It's clean and simple, containing the following apparatus:

A sink (an ingenious device that helps remove tar, dirt and 40-weight engine oil from under the fingernails—Real Men, after all, are not afraid to get their hands dirty).

An oven (a concession to modern times, since most Real Men have removed the open pit, finding that the smoke tends to ruin the mirrors on their bedroom ceilings).

A refrigerator (which will preserve not only fresh meat, but also such critical Real Men paraphernalia as 35-mm film, small batteries, beer and ice packs for the occasional football injury).

And, finally, the Real Man's kitchen always contains steak knives (tax deductible under the heading "home security devices").

But equally important is what you won't find in the Real Man's kitchen.

Needless to say, the refrigerator will not contain Lo-Cal yogurt dressing.

There will be no cutesy fruit-shaped magnets stuck on the refrigerator door, nor will there be such trivial items as cat calendars, diets clipped from a newspaper, shopping lists, or cents-off coupons on asparagus, veal cordon bleu or the latest mocha-flavored coffee.

(Generally speaking, the only time a Real Man uses a coupon is for charcoal briquettes. Real Men believe newspapers are for news, sports and stock-market reports; they don't have time to peruse the food section in order to save 15¢ on Ty-D-bol.)

But this is only the beginning.

Inside the Real Man's kitchen you will find no chopsticks, napkin rings, demitasse spoons, ornate fruit cups, silver tea servers or vegetable steamers.

There will be no matching service for eight.

There will be no Fitz and Floyd china.

There will be no Flintstones drinking glasses. (This is admittedly a sad concession, but it's an important rite of passage nevertheless.)

Ok—I can't take anymore. Here's Don Corleone's recipe for linguini with red clam sauce.

And the Real Man's kitchen contains no aprons, lobster bibs, vitamins, wheat germ, placemats or hanging plants.

In terms of hardware, Real Men do not take the easy way out with faddish convenience devices.

Real Men do not own hot-doggers, electric woks, or FryBaby, espresso machines, popcorn makers, salad spinners, convection ovens, pasta machines, Toast-r-ovens, coffee grinders or electric garbage disposals; and they certainly don't own cuisinarts or Veg-o-matics.

(Actually, Real Men think the best use of an electric garbage disposal took place in the movie *Rolling Thunder*, when a group of thugs shoved William Devane's hand down one for retribution. The screenwriter will no doubt defend this as some kind of deep sociopsychological metaphor—but Real Men appreciate it for the cheap, trite, gratuitous violence and sensationalism it really was.)

Given the choice, a Real Man would always rather hack, cut, slice, dice, mince and chop his way through life with Sheffield steel knives. (Not to mention the fact that if something needs to be stirred or cut beyond the capacity of a Real Man's arms, he'll take the food in question down to his workshop, where he already owns a drill press and buzz saw.)

Of course, there is *one* convenience item no Real Man can do without:

An ice maker.

Because, as we all know, you never have enough ice.

Real Man
Cooking Lesson #3

Q. What does a Real Man use
a wok for?

A. Oil changes.

5

Breakfast

Let's face it:
The Army Corps of Engineers does not go to work on a belly filled with crepes.

And neither should you.

Yes, it's an undeniable fact that a Real Man needs a Real Breakfast in the morning.

And it doesn't matter whether you're a stockbroker in Manhattan who's about to be indicted for inside trading or the member of the Army Corps of Engineers who's responsible for wiping out the snail darter, because the simple truth is that *every* Real Man needs a hearty breakfast—not only to build up his stamina for the day ahead, but also to help him recover from his sexual acrobatics the night before.

With this in mind, it should be obvious that Real Men do not begin their day with warm milk.

Real Men do not eat brunch.

They do not eat eggs hussard.

And they certainly don't start off the day with croissants, Cream of Wheat, peach yogurt or any kind of children's breakfast cereal that has pictures of cartoon characters on the box.

(Real Men understand that anyone who begins the day staring at a box of Froot Loops or Cocoa Puffs will hardly be in the right frame of mind to stare down a hostile board of directors in the corporate conference room.)

So what *do* Real Men eat in the morning?

They eat donuts.

Kaiser rolls.

They eat slabs o' bacon, sides o' fries and stacks o' flaps.

And they love to consume vast quantities of wheat cakes, griddlecakes, pancakes, sausage and anything that would ordinarily be found on the menu at the International House of Pancakes.

(Real Men, you see, recognize that John Glenn did not become the first American to orbit the earth by eating a breakfast of grapefruit and cottage cheese.)

If you're confused about what to eat in the morning, the following may help:

If a certain breakfast dish seems as though it might be best suited for people like John Davidson, Gary Collins or Dick Van Patten, pass on it immediately.

But if, on the other hand, the food seems like it might be enjoyed by Richard Boone, Brock Yates, Ellston Howard, Broderick Crawford, Harrison Ford, Paul Harvey, Lee Iacocca, Tim Matheson, Johnny Cash or Ricki Lee Jones, it's a good bet you're on the right track.

Perfect Scrambled Eggs

Every Real Man loves eggs for breakfast—because it requires breaking them in the process of cooking.

(Put in more psychological terms, what could be better for a Real Man's spirit at 6 o'clock in the morning than the notion that he can beat mother nature?)

INGREDIENTS
  3 *large eggs*
    butter
    *club soda**

To begin, break the eggs into a large bowl and beat them until thoroughly mixed.

(If you ordinarily avoid this kind of manual labor, don't worry; merely view it as therapeutic exercise and pretend the eggs represent OSHA, Bowie Kuhn or your dry cleaner.)

Next, melt several tablespoons of butter into a large frying pan over a medium flame.

When the butter begins to smoke, add a shot of club soda to the egg mixture.

Then pour the mix into the frying pan, before the butter burns, and cook to taste.

The Morning-After Omelet

As we all know, everyone wakes up famished.

But as we also all know, there's nothing more clichéd than offering to buy your date breakfast.

Thus, the morning-after omelet.

A perfect way to show a woman you're well rounded—and can exhibit the same prowess in the

---

*The club soda makes the eggs lighter and fluffier. For an interesting variation, you can substitute champagne left over from the night before.

kitchen that you exhibited in the bedroom the night before.

INGREDIENTS

    8 *extra-large eggs*
    1 *large green pepper*
    1 *large onion*
    1 *pound cooked ham*
  ½ *pound cheddar cheese*
  ½ *pound Swiss cheese*
    1 *large tomato*

First, chop the pepper, onion, tomato and ham into small pieces. (Red peppers, salami, mushrooms or anything else that seems vaguely edible in your refrigerator may be substituted.)

Second, beat the eggs in a bowl and add in all the chopped ingredients except for the cheese.

Next, melt several tablespoons of butter into a frying pan over a medium flame. . . . And when the butter begins to smoke, pour the entire mixture into the pan.

When the concoction is half cooked, place the cheeses on top of the omelet and cover the entire frying pan with a pot top.

Cook for a minute or two until the cheese melts, then add seasoning to taste.

Yield: 3 servings.

NOTE: Among the cognoscenti, this is known as a garbage omelet, because it will not only impress your date but also use up any excess food in your refrigerator before it becomes moldy and begins to look like a failed science project.

Feel free to experiment and substitute things like leftover spaghetti sauce for cheese or, for the meat, try using the steak or lobster your date brought home from the restaurant in a doggie bag the night before.

Beyond this, in order to ensure the perfect romantic breakfast, just add American Country Bis-

cuits (see recipe on page 37), orange juice, blueber-
ries, any champagne left over from the night before—
and the Sunday morning papers. (Especially if it's
Saturday morning. She'll be amazed at your re-
sourcefulness.)

Do remember one thing, however: No woman is
impressed by Sara Lee pound cake served out of a
half-crushed tin.

Ham Steak and Redeye Gravy

Imagine you're in Bismarck, North Dakota. It's dawn.
The dead of winter. The snow is so high you can
barely see over the basketball net in your driveway;
the temperature is 50 degrees below zero. Inside the
house.

This is the time for ham steak and redeye gravy.

You don't live in Bismarck, North Dakota?

It doesn't matter.

Because even if you reside in such quiche-eating
locales as Palm Springs, Palm Beach, or Wilton, Con-
necticut, one thing always remains the same:

In the cold, cruel, dog-eat-dog world of Real Men,
every morning is 6 o'clock in the morning in the
middle of December in Bismarck, North Dakota.

INGREDIENTS

  *1 pound country ham steak
     black coffee*

Start by cooking the ham steak slowly in a large
skillet until tender—about 15 minutes.

Once this is finished, remove the ham and add 1½
cups of water to the skillet.

Bring the water to a boil and scrape all the cooking
particles and red meat from the bottom of the pan;

boil for several more minutes (until the mixture begins to thicken) and add several tablespoons of black coffee to darken and add taste to the gravy.

Serve with scrambled eggs and home fries—liberally pouring the gravy on the fries and ham steak.

Yield: 2 servings

Old-Fashioned Buttermilk Pancakes

Aunt Jemima may be good, but these are better.

INGREDIENTS
- 4 *eggs*
- 6 *cups buttermilk*
- 2 *tablespoons sugar*
- 2½ *teaspoons baking soda*
- 1 *teaspoon salt*
- ½ *cup melted butter*

Beat the eggs in a bowl and add the buttermilk.

Mix, then pour the dry ingredients into the batter while stirring constantly. Continue stirring until the batter is smooth. If the batter is too thick to pour, add water.

Next, add the melted butter to the batter.

Heat a frying pan on a medium flame and prime with a tablespoon of butter.

Once the butter is bubbling, add the batter half a cup at a time to make man-sized flapjacks.

As soon as bubbles begin to appear on the surface of the batter, flip the pancake once.

Yield: 20 pancakes—enough for 2 members of any Alabama road gang.

NOTE: Use only pure maple syrup—the kind preferred by lumberjacks everywhere.

Mining Camp Potatoes

Every man needs a shot of starch in the morning.
And not just in his shirts.

INGREDIENTS

1¼ pound raw bacon, diced
6 potatoes, cut into man-sized chunks
½ cup onion, chopped beyond recognition
1½ teaspoons salt
¼ teaspoon pepper

In a large skillet, cook the bacon until crisp.

Remove the bacon from the pan, but do not drain
the fat.

Put the remaining ingredients into the bacon fat
and toss them for two minutes over a high flame.

Return the cooked bacon to the skillet and *slowly*
add warm water until the potatoes are three-quarters covered.

Finally, cover the pan and cook over a medium
flame for 20 minutes.

(Admittedly, this is not as fast as McDonald's. But
if it took 20 million years to create a masterpiece like
the Grand Canyon, surely you can wait 20 minutes
for great spuds.)

Yield: 4 servings

Rocky Mountain Toast

For years, people who've watched television have had
a simple set of questions:

What did Tonto feed the Lone Ranger?

What did Butch feed Sundance?

What did Cheyenne feed Sugarfoot?

What did Johnny feed the Rifleman?

What did Chester feed Matt Dillon?

What did Ben feed Hoss?

And—most importantly—what did Paladin feed
himself?

To be honest, we don't know.

But we strongly suspect that if these brave, upstanding men had started their day with Rocky Mountain toast, they would have lived to die in gun battles, instead of getting killed in the ratings.

INGREDIENTS

3 *pieces sourdough bread*
4 *eggs*
1 *stick butter*
2 *pieces Canadian bacon*

Melt two tablespoons of butter in a skillet.

Take one slice of the bacon and sauté it over a low flame until brown. (Note: For those of you not intimately familiar with the cuisine of our friends to the north, Canadian bacon looks like a salami. And try not to remember that this is the country that gave us a quiche-eater like Pierre Trudeau—because it also gave us the National Hockey League.)

Now that you've finished musing about international politics, remove the bacon from the skillet and set it aside on a paper towel.

Next, take a piece of sourdough bread. Take a water glass, turn it upside down and punch a hole in the center of the bread.

(Don't get carried away here and use such alternatives as a drill press, 12-gauge shotgun or—perish the thought—chain saw.)

To continue, place the bread in the skillet and brown it in the bacon fat and butter.

Once the bread is browned on one side, flip it over. (If the skillet is dry, add another tablespoon of butter.)

Let the other side of the bread brown for a minute. Once this is finished, crack an egg and place it in the center of the bread—as if you were making a sunny-side-up egg.

As soon as the egg firms up, place the bacon on top.

Quickly flip the toast over to momentarily reheat the bacon, and serve.

Yield: 2 servings

United Auto Workers Donuts

Respectfully Dedicated
to Ralph Cramden
(and Norton)

Taste these and you'll understand why the A.F. of L.-C.I.O. has always negotiated for longer coffee breaks.

INGREDIENTS
    1 *package dry yeast (1 tablespoon)*
    6 *tablespoons warm water*
    1 *cup lukewarm milk*
    2 *cups flour*

Start by dissolving the yeast in the water in a large bowl. Once the yeast is *completely* dissolved, add the remaining ingredients.

Cover the bowl with a towel and place it in a warm, draft-free area. Let the mixture rise for 45 minutes.

(A warm, draft-free area is the top of your stove—*not* southern Florida.)

Now, take the following and with your hands mix into another large bowl:

    6 *cups flour*
    1 *cup sugar*
    1 *teaspoon salt*
 1½ *cups softened butter*
    6 *eggs*
    ¼ *cup milk*

After these ingredients are fully mixed, slowly add 2 cups of warm milk, mixing constantly until you have a soft dough.

Stir in the yeast mixture (the thing that's not sitting in Key Biscayne) and knead the dough for several minutes.

Just to pass the time, here's a joke you may tell while you're doing this:

Question: What does a Real Man play on the piano?
Answer: Poker.

With the entertainment segment of the recipe completed, on a lightly floured board, roll the dough into cylinders four inches long and three-quarters of an inch wide.

Bring the ends of the cylinders together to form the donuts.

Next (and finally) lay the donuts out on a cookie sheet and let them rise until they are double their size.

With this completed, *fill* a *deep* pan with cooking oil, leaving 2 inches of room at the top, and heat to 375 degrees.

With a spatula, gently slide the donuts in and cook until golden brown.

Yield: 3 dozen

Bring Me the Plate of Alfredo Garcia Sausage

If there is truly a Real Man's grande cuisine, this is it. What caviar is to lesser mortals, this is to Real Men.

It may take longer to prepare—but, like World War II, it's worth the struggle.

Before you start this recipe, go to a butcher and have him grind one pound of pork fat and two pounds of fresh lean pork meat together. Ham, loin or shoulder will suffice.

(You can do this at home if you have a meat grinder, cyclotron, paper shredder, or—heaven forgive us— if you wife owns a Cuisinart.)

Fire's ok, but I still prefer to thaw it and eat it.

Next, prepare the following Alfredo Garcia sausage spice:

> 1 *tablespoon crushed bay leaves*
> 1 *tablespoon ground clove*
> 1 *tablespoon mace (the spice, not the riot deterrent)*
> 1 *tablespoon nutmeg*
> 1 *tablespoon paprika*
> 1 *tablespoon thyme*
> 1½ *teaspoons basil*
> 1½ *teaspoons cinnamon*
> 1½ *teaspoons oregano*
> 1½ *teaspoons sage*
> 1½ *teaspoons savory*
> ½ *cup white peppercorns*

Grind all these ingredients together—using a coffee mill, Cuisinart, blender or spice mill.

Take two teaspoons of Al's spice (Real Men can call each other by their nicknames), add one tablespoon of salt and beat it into the ground meat.

(With all the grinding and beating, it's no wonder this is named after Alfredo Garcia.)

Now cover the mixture and place it in the refrigerator for a minimum of 12 hours.

(In the interim defend the Alamo, or just teach someone a lesson.)

Welcome back.

Now the serious cooking begins.

Cover the bottom of a frying pan with a half inch of water.

Form the sausage mixture into small patties and cook over a low flame 10 minutes or more, until cooked through.

IMPORTANT NOTE: Make *sure* the patties are cooked all the way through. Real Men can think of better things to die of than trichinosis.

Yield: 16 patties

American Country Biscuits

What the Pillsbury doughboy would have baked—if only he'd been the Pillsbury dough man.

INGREDIENTS

- 2 *cups flour*
- 2½ *teaspoons double-acting baking powder*
- 2 *teaspoons sugar*
- 1 *teaspoon salt*
- 7 *tablespoons butter*
- ¾ *cup milk*

First, play reveille for your family.

Second, preheat the oven to 375°, then combine all the dry ingredients in a large bowl.

Cut the butter into small bits and stir them into the dry ingredients, using your finger tips to make sure it's well combined.

Next, slowly add the milk to the mixture while stirring continually.

Once all the milk has been added, knead the dough for one minute until smooth.

Roll the dough out to quarter-inch thickness.

Cut into squares and place on a dry cookie sheet.

Place the cookie sheet on the middle shelf.

Bake for 12 minutes, and feel secure knowing you've passed on a small piece of America's heritage to your children.

Yield: 2 dozen

Well, well—a three martini lunch. Joey Martini,
Al Martini, and Nick, "The Pliers," Martini.

6

Lunch

It's midday.

You've topped out a 70-story skyscraper, moved an 18-wheeler 1,000 miles, engineered the unfriendly takeover of a Fortune 500 company and loaded enough boxcars to stretch from here to Shreveport and back again.

No, this is not time for Miller.

It's time for lunch.

And contrary to the rantings and ravings of Congress, we're not talking about a simple dignified Blimpie Tuna on White #2.

No way.

The subject under discussion here is the fabulous three-martini, all-expenses-paid, slush-fund, American Express, IRS, expense-account extravaganza. The kind of meal that starts at noon and runs till 4:30; the kind of eating binge that keeps eminent cardiologists in business; the kind of lunch that manipulates stock prices, fixes union problems or puts you in partnership with Don King.

So why, you may ask, is Congress so upset with the three-martini lunch?

It could be they prefer to start drinking before noon.

Or it may just be another example of our government's colossal misunderstanding of the way American business works.*

*In the early 1800s, the French writer Alexis de Tocqueville was the first to point out that second-raters tend to run for political office in America—while the best and the brightest are attracted to the risks, rewards and challenges of commerce. De Tocqueville came to this conclusion after meeting various American politicians over lunch and dinner—all of which he is reputed to have "put in" for. Had de Tocqueville been alive today, we're reasonably certain he would have postulated that Real Men create their own destiny—while Congressmen seem to do nothing but muck everyone else's up.

Either way, however, we feel it's time that somebody set the world straight about this meal.

The American business lunch is the perfect time to exert undue influence on a union shop steward, set up a merger that will drive the Securities and Exchange Commission wild or just look for another job.

It is *not* the time for white wine, fruit compote, poached salmon in a light dill sauce or a waiter who approaches your table by saying, "Hi. My name is David, and I'll be serving you today." (To this, Real Men always reply, "Hi. My name is Vic, and I'll be leaving you now.")

Real Men, you see, understand there is no such thing as a free lunch—but they have absolutely no compunction about letting Uncle Sam underwrite a large portion of it.

This is not to say, however, that everyone has exactly the same perspective on this meal.

When Armand Hammer (chairman of the board of Occidental Petroleum) says he's going out for a business lunch, it usually means he's going to swallow an entire industry.

Harry Truman "chewed out" Douglas MacArthur.

And when Anthony "Tony Pro" Provenzano talks about "talkin' turkey," other people get indigestion.

But no matter what, there is one simple, fundamental truth about the Real Man's lunch.

At noon, a Real Man needs a meal with legs on it. He needs something that will stick to his ribs, not merely to the roof of his mouth.

And whether it's delivered in a lunch pail, off the back of a canteen truck, or on a silver platter at the 21 Club, one thing is certain:

The day is yet young, and a Real Man needs nourishment.

Because there are still breeder reactors to fix, lawsuits to file, Chevys to call back and lots of important police work ahead.

Real Man
Cooking Quiz #1

Q. Where does a Real Man eat in San Francisco?

A. He eats in Oakland.

The Battle of Atlanta Fried Chicken

If nothing else, the Civil War was, well, civil. They always broke for lunch. And, more often than not, they ate fried chicken.

The following recipe uses a peach sauce that was originated in the grand hotels of Atlanta. The dish is spicier than most of the frozen commercial varieties we've grown used to, but if anyone complains, just say, "Frankly, my dear, I don't give a damn."

Especially if it's a man.

INGREDIENTS

2 cut-up chickens
2 cups milk
1 teaspoon Tabasco sauce
2 cups flour
1½ teaspoons salt
2 fresh hot red peppers, chopped fine
½ gallon of Planters Peanut Oil
A deep frying pan
One unsoiled brown grocery bag

To start, mix the milk and Tabasco sauce in a large bowl. Place the chicken parts into the bowl and refrigerate for at least one hour.

(If you don't have a watch, four innings of a baseball game, one period of hockey or one short phone call to your mother should suffice.)

Next, put the flour, salt and red pepper into the grocery bag. Clutch the bag at the top and shake to combine the ingredients.

Next, fill the frying pan with oil until it comes within one and a half inches of the top. Heat the oil over a medium flame until it just barely smokes.

At this point, remove the chicken from the refrigerator and drop it into the bag one piece at a time.

Shake the bag to make sure the chicken is completely coated.

Gently place the chicken in the oil, making sure not to splatter yourself.

Fry until golden brown—and cooked inside, about 8 to 10 minutes. During the cooking process, regulate the flame to make sure the chicken does not burn.

Serve smothered with the following Georgia peach sauce:

GEORGIA PEACH SAUCE INGREDIENTS

 1 8-ounce jar of peach preserves
 ¼ cup of water
 1 medium onion, sliced
 4 tablespoons butter
 ½ teaspoon paprika
 juice of one lemon
 1 tablespoon white vinegar
 1 tablespoon brown sugar
 ½ teaspoon Worcestershire sauce

Combine all the ingredients in a saucepan and bring to a boil.

Turn down the heat and simmer (partially covered) for 10 minutes.

Once you've tasted this, you too will wonder how the South lost.

Yield: 6 servings

Hamburger

Alas, the quiching of America has reached the hamburger.

Unfortunately, it seems that every two-bit salad-and-yogurt joint in the country has found it necessary to come up with a different name for this dish.

And with things like Alpine burgers, Rancho burgers, Big Macs, Whoppers, Grand Wizard of the KKK burgers and Salisbury steak, can Bill Blass burgers be far behind?

By the Real Man's way of thinking, this is, well, stupid.

A hamburger is a hamburger. And there's only one acceptable variation: the bacon cheeseburger.

They're America's holy food, and no World Series, poker game, or first teen-age date would be complete without them. (In fact, it's even been suggested that Uncle Sam should pass them out to Democratic converts the way the Pope hands out holy wafers.)

Now, admittedly, the following recipe may be more interesting and tasty than most.

But for Real Men, the idea of inventing a cute name for it would be blasphemy. Or treason.

Or, worse, it would be like trying to come up with a different name for the Jeep.

INGREDIENTS
- 4 *slices of bacon*
- 2 *quarter-pound hamburger patties—flavored to taste with A-1 sauce and Tabasco sauce, plus salt and pepper*
- 2 *slices American cheese*
- 1 *half-inch-thick slice Bermuda onion*

First, fry the bacon in a skillet until crisp.

Next, remove the bacon from the pan and fry the hamburger patties in the remaining bacon fat.

When the burgers are done on one side, flip them and place a slice of cheese on the cooked side of each burger.

By the time the patty is cooked on the opposite side, the cheese will be melted, and you're ready to construct the finished burger:

Do this:

Place one patty on the bottom half of a hamburger bun, cheese side up.

Place the onion and bacon on top.

Then place the other patty on top of that, cheese side down.

Crown with the top of the bun.

China Syndrome Chili

A recipe guaranteed to melt down your stomach.

INGREDIENTS

2	pounds beef chuck, cut into cubes
½	cup vegetable oil
2	onions, chopped
4	cloves garlic, chopped
1	small can of tomato paste
1	small can of tomato sauce
4	chili peppers
1	large pinch cayenne pepper
2	tablespoons paprika
2	teaspoons oregano
4	teaspoons cumin
	salt to taste
1–2	cans pinto beans

In a large skillet, heat the oil until it's smoking hot. In two batches, brown the beef on all sides and drain the oil from the pan.

Cover the beef with water, cover the skillet and simmer over a low flame for 90 minutes.

(Note: during this entire process, make sure the chili does not come to a boil, or burn.)

Add onions; simmer for a half-hour, covered.

Following this, add the remaining ingredients and simmer an additional half-hour, uncovered.

Top with either homemade or canned pinto beans.*

Yell, "Come and get it."

Yield: 4 servings.

*To make homemade pinto beans, take a pound of dried pinto beans, cover with water and let soak overnight. Place the beans in a fresh pot, cover with water, add a tablespoon of salt, one chopped onion, one red chili pepper and two bay leaves. Simmer slowly until tender.

Samuelson's Economic Pizza

Remember Economics 101?

Remember the way you could never make sense out of the pie graphs?

The explanation for this lack of understanding is simple: We were a generation brought up on pizza pie—not the apple variety.

With this recipe, you'll garner firsthand knowledge of the following critical economic principles:

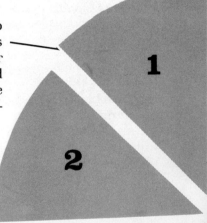

Demand pull inflation. As you go back to repurchase the ingredients over the next few years, you'll see their prices keep going up. (Often referred to as "the more you want it, the more it costs" theory of modern economics.)

Class structure. This is an egalitarian pie, with both a lower and upper crust.

Division of labor. The person who rings up your groceries will never be the person who bags them.

Price supports. Thanks to our government's dairy-support system, you'll notice the cheese is priced at an artificially high level.

Microeconomics. If you'd like, this can be cooked in an extremely expensive microwave—teaching you about research-and-development costs, finance payments and multibillion-dollar class-action suits from people who've caught radiation poisoning from them.

5

Balance of trade payments. With the cost of the nuclear reactors we've been shipping to Italy, the imported olive oil in this recipe will hardly put a dent in their trade deficit—but at least it's a nice gesture.

6

The American distribution system. One store will never have everything you need.

7

M-1, B-1 and the Federal Reserve Board. First, as with all things economic, this recipe deals with dough. Second, thanks to the Federal Reserve Board, come Friday night somebody will always have enough cash on hand to purchase the ingredients.

8

Capitalism. Once you've tasted this pizza, you'll understand—once and for all—the basic motivation in American Society:

9

Everybody wants a bigger piece of the pie.

Now that you've mastered economics, here's how to master the pizza.

PIZZA INGREDIENTS
(for one 10-inch pizza)
    1 *pizza dough (see following recipe)*
    ½ *cup pizza sauce (see following recipe)*
    ½ *cup grated mozzarella cheese*
    2 *tablespoons grated Parmesan cheese*
    2 *tablespoons imported olive oil*

Preheat oven to 550 degrees.

Take half of the pizza dough and roll it out into a circle 10 inches wide and one-eighth of an inch thick.

With the tips of your fingers, work your way around the dough, crimping the perimeter to form a rim.

Lightly dust a baking sheet with flour and place the dough on it. Pour the pizza sauce into the center, swirling it around with the back of a spoon until evenly distributed.

Sprinkle the cheeses on the pizza, dribble the oil on the top and garnish with anything you'd like, including sausage, pepperoni, meatballs, anchovies, mushrooms, onions or garlic.

Finally, take the completed pie and bake on the lowest shelf of your oven for 10 minutes, or until the pizza sauce is bubbling and the crust is brown.

PIZZA DOUGH INGREDIENTS
(for two 10-inch pizzas)
    1 *package dry yeast*
       pinch of sugar
    ¼ *cup lukewarm water*

Put the water into a small bowl and dissolve the dry ingredients into it. Wait several minutes until the mixture doubles in volume.

1¾ *cups all-purpose flour*
½ *teaspoon salt*

Sift these dry ingredients into a large bowl and add the yeast mixture to it.

½ *cup lukewarm water*
⅛ *cup olive oil*

Using your hands, mix the liquids into the flour and gather into a rough ball. Place the dough on a lightly floured board and knead it for 10 minutes.

Next, dust the dough with flour, place it in a bowl, cover it with a towel and move it to a warm, draft-free area. Let the dough rise for 90 minutes—or until it doubles its bulk.

PIZZA SAUCE INGREDIENTS
1½ *tablespoons oil*
1½ *tablespoons finely chopped garlic*

In a medium saucepan, slowly sauté the garlic in oil for two minutes.

Then add the following ingredients to the pan:

2 *cups canned tomatoes with their juice*
3 *ounces tomato paste*
1½ *teaspoons oregano*
1½ *teaspoons basil*
1 *teaspoon sugar*
½ *bay leaf*
¾ *teaspoon salt*
black pepper to taste

Once you've mixed these ingredients thoroughly, bring the mixture to a boil, turn the heat down very low and simmer for 45 minutes, stirring occasionally with a wooden spoon.

The sauce should be quite thick when finished.

Felix Frankfurter Hot Dogs

Real Men do not sit on the bench during baseball, football or hockey games; but they *do*, however, sit on the bench of the Supreme Court.

Admittedly, there is no evidence that Felix Frankfurter ever ate hot dogs. But one thing is indisputable:

This is a precedent-setting recipe. And no matter what your particular interpretation may be, it will do wonders for any Real Man's constitution.

Justice, after all, may be blind, but that doesn't mean it also has to go hungry.

INGREDIENTS

*1 American country biscuit dough (see recipe
page 37)
hot dogs
your favorite relishes
mustard
coarsely grated cheddar cheese
poppy seeds*

Take the hot dogs and slit them open lengthwise, approximately three-quarters of the way through.

Fill the slit with mustard, relish, cheese, onions, sauerkraut or any combination thereof.

Next, take the biscuit dough, place it on your kitchen counter and roll it out to a one-eighth-inch thickness.

Cut the dough into rectangles wide enough to completely wrap the hot dogs, while leaving the ends of the meat exposed.

(Make sure the dough is pinched together at the seam, or it will unravel during cooking.)

Place the poppy seeds on a plate and roll the dogs in them.

Finally, place the dogs on a lightly oiled cookie sheet and bake on the top shelf of your oven for 12 minutes at 450 degrees—or until the dough is nicely browned.

Serve on the first Monday in October.

Real Man Cooking
Quiz #2

 Q. Why do Real Men eat out?

 A. On the off chance they may have to perform the Heimlich maneuver during dinner.

"Ted can't enjoy a picnic 'till he's secured the perimeter against ants."

7

Lunch Side Dishes

Real Men have always had something on the side.
Whether it's side arms, side bets, aluminum
siding, Valerie Perrine or a sidekick, it's the way Real
Men spice up their lives.

The same logic can be applied to a Real Man's
meals.

To a Real Man, a hamburger without fries is like
Mantle without Maris.

A ham sandwich without pickles is like Carson
without McMahon.

And a meatball hero without chips is like Mobil
Oil without a corporate acquisition policy.

This is not to say, however, that just any garnish
will do.

Real Men do not put parsley on the side of anything.

They do not augment their sandwiches with orange slices, radish rosettes or cherry tomatoes.

And a Real Man will never eat anything skewered
with a frilly toothpick.

When it comes to side dishes, only the following
will suffice.

Nat King Cole Slaw

(Prepared to the tune of the "Christmas Song," this salad should be eaten while watching *Cat Ballou*.)

INGREDIENTS

1   *head of red cabbage, shredded*
1   *onion, grated*
2   *green peppers, grated*
2   *cloves garlic, finely chopped*
3   *tablespoons melted oil*
3   *tablespoons lemon juice*
2   *tablespoons chopped chives*
2   *tablespoons chopped parsley*
   *pinch cayenne pepper, plus salt and pepper to
      taste*

Yield: 6–8 servings

Cabbage shredded on your kitchen counter,
Onions nipping at your nose.

Your grater sounds like an infected choir;
For garlic, please chop up two cloves.

Everybody knows green pepper makes your slaw complete,
While cayenne helps to bring some spice.

Tiny chives, chopped up fine in a bowl;
Add salt and pepper, parsley, till right.

You know the dish is almost done.
Add melted butter, lemons for some fun.

And when you mix it up in a bowl,
You know it's best not to serve too cold.

And so, we're offering this simple dish,
For kids from one to 92.

For though it's been said, many times, many ways,

Happy cole slaw
To you.

Offshore Drilling Platform Potato Salad

Let's face it:

When you're out in the ocean battling the wind, fighting the drill and trying to duck some half-crazed Vietnam vet helicopter jock, you don't need arugola salad.

You need a salad with ballast.

Something that will keep you on board—even when the rig itself tips over, causing untold ecological damage.

INGREDIENTS

2½ pounds new potatoes, washed. Do not peel.
6 shallots, peeled and sliced.
¾ cup cheap white wine
4 tablespoons hot mustard
1 tablespoon red wine vinegar
¾ cup oil

First, place the potatoes in a large pot of boiling water.

While the potatoes are boiling, do the following:

Place the shallots and white wine in a small saucepan. Boil rapidly (over a high flame) until the wine is two-thirds evaporated and the shallots are soft.

Meanwhile, back at the first pot, once the potatoes are soft enough to be easily pierced by a fork, remove them and chill them in your refrigerator.

Next, prepare the following dressing:

In a small bowl, beat the vinegar into the mustard. Add the oil very slowly, while beating constantly until the dressing is as thick as mayonnaise.

Once the potatoes are thoroughly chilled, slice and toss in a large bowl with the dressing and the shallots.

Serve—but try to keep the dish covered in the event you hit a gusher.

Yield: 4 servings

Casablanca Baked Beans

Because, "I'm no good at being noble but it doesn't take much to see that the problems of three little people don't amount to a hill o' beans in this crazy world."

INGREDIENTS

3 *cups white pea beans*
1½ *teaspoons salt*
2 *onions, roughly chopped*
8 *pork spareribs*
5 *ounces molasses*
3 *teaspoons dry mustard*
1½ *teaspoons black pepper*

Start by soaking the beans in tap water for five hours. Then drain them and place them in a large pot.

In the new pot, cover the beans with fresh water and add salt. Simmer over a low flame for 40 minutes, until the beans are just barely tender. Then drain well. Preheat oven to 250 degrees.

Place the onions and spareribs in a large oven-proof dish. Add the beans and cover the mixture with boiling water. Stir in the molasses; add the mustard and pepper.

Cover and bake for five hours.

NOTE: Check the beans often, adding water as necessary to make sure the mixture is covered.

Yield: 6–8 servings

Real Man Cooking Lesson #4 Three Ways to Call a Real Man to the Dinner Table

1. "Chow time."

2. "Soup's on."

3. "Isn't 'Little House on the Prairie' about to start on TV?"

8. Great Moments in

The Garden of Eden.
Adam proves once
and for all
that fruit
has no place in
the Real Man's diet.

1100
The Poles
invent vodka.

1837
Oliver Twist
asks for seconds.

33 A.D.
The Last Supper.
Real Men devise
the first
retirement dinner.

985
John Barleycorn
appears in
England.

1899
Colonel Sanders
is born.

1400
A "Mrs. Polo"
refuses to cook
on Sunday night.
Her husband, Marco,
goes out
for Chinese food.

1,000,000 B.C.
Lightning strikes
a pterodactyl,
instantly frying it.
Real Men sample
remains and comment:
"Mmmmm. Tastes
just like chicken."

Real Man Cuisine

1957
Nixon
meets Khrushchev
in the kitchen.

1977
Sylvester Stallone
eats raw eggs
for breakfast
in *Rocky I*.
Earns $300 million
at the box office.

1927
The Palm
restaurant
opens in
New York.

1972
Richard Castellano
gives the recipe
for spaghetti sauce
in *The Godfather*.*

1972
Deep Throat
is released.

1944
Patton
wins the Battle
of the Bulge.
Says "It was
no picnic."

1981
Burger King introduces
"specialty sandwiches,"
thus inventing
the Real Man's
nouvelle cuisine.

1962
Mothra eats
Tokyo.

*See page 73 for complete details.

An apple! I gave up a perfectly good rib for an apple?

9

Dinner

After a hard day working on the parole board, fighting alligators at Sea World or just destroying people's credit for late payments at the bank, your wife (or girlfriend) deserves a break.

And we're not talking about McDonald's.

As surprising as it may seem, Real Men cook dinner for their loved ones. There are three simple reasons for this:

First, they do it because it helps them avoid doing the dishes.

Second, because there are only so many nights you can eat hamburgers.

And, third, because there's no better setting than champagne and candlelight to coax a girl into bed, or to tell her you're breaking up.

(Admittedly, this may seem a little cynical, but consider this: Where would *you* rather face Barbara Walters? At a 7:30 breakfast in a greasy spoon on Sixth Avenue, a 12:30 lunch in a chichi restaurant where Jacques the maitre d' kisses her hello or a 9:00 tête-à-tête in your apartment?)

Summing up, dinner is the ideal time for romance and seduction.

It's the perfect way to impress a woman—and allows you to show off your collection of "important 20th-century cultural works," such as your $300,000 stereo system, clean designer sheets and 16-foot Advent television set. (It's also the perfect time to impress her with your American Express gold card, although this is much more difficult to work into the conversation.)

Needless to say, all of this is irrelevant if Muhammad Ali happens to be making a comeback on HBO this particular evening.

But if he isn't, sit back, turn down the lights, chill the champagne and slap a Sinatra album on the turntable.

With luck, you'll never get to the food.

Little Caesar Salad

"Now listen up, pal.

"You just can't jump into a steak dinner with some broad and expect things to work out, ya see?

"You gotta ease into things. You gotta take it slow. You gotta work with finesse. And style. Like the way Frank Nitti moved in on Capone's Cicero operations in 1929. Or the way that the Tattaglias muscled in on Vito Corleone in '56.

"So that's why I'm giving you this recipe.

"A lot of people think it's named after some Italian guy, Julius Caesar. But they're wrong, see? He was a pansy. They wrote plays about him. He ran around in a toga. No wonder his friends bumped him off.

"So listen, and listen tight, ya mugs.

"This salad is named after me. It's good. Real good. And nobody crosses Little Caesar.

"So try it, see?"

CROUTON INGREDIENTS

> ½ cup imported olive oil
> 3 cloves chopped garlic
> 4 cups cubed crustless white bread

Heat the oil in a skillet until it is smoking hot. Add the garlic, sauté for one minute and then add the bread until golden brown.

SALAD INGREDIENTS

> 4 heads romaine lettuce
> dry mustard, salt and pepper
> 1 cup grated Parmesan cheese
> ⅜ cup imported olive oil
> juice of four lemons
> 4 eggs
> 8 slices of cooked, crips bacon
> 8 chopped anchovy fillets

Tear the lettuce into pieces and place in a very large bowl. Sprinkle with mustard, salt and pepper to taste. Add the Parmesan cheese and toss lightly.

Next, add the lemon juice and oil. Break the eggs onto the lettuce and toss lightly. All the leaves should be coated.

Finally top with crumbled bacon and anchovies. Add croutons, toss well and serve immediately.

Yield: 8 servings

Cream of Beer Soup

By its very nature, soup is not generally considered a Real Man's dish.

It cannot be barbecued. You can't eat it on a bun. It has no bones, cannot be ordered well done, and a steak knife will be useless in its consumption.

Yet, despite this bad news, soup remains an essential ingredient in any romantic dinner.

Thus we offer cream of beer soup.

Admittedly, it's not as Real Man-ish as 'gator bisque. But at least it won't put off women, and surely it's better than starting off your meal with dry-roasted peanuts.

INGREDIENTS

>   3 *tablespoons unsalted butter*
>   ½ *large head of cabbage, shredded fine*
>   1 *large onion, chopped fine*
>   1 *tablespoon flour*
>   2 *cups canned chicken broth*
>   2 *cups beer**
>   *salt and pepper*
>   ½ *cup cream*
>   ½ *cup milk*

Melt the butter in a 4 quart pot. Add the cabbage and onions and cook them until soft. Then sprinkle the mixture with the flour and cook for one minute longer, stirring constantly.

Add the broth, beer and salt and pepper (to taste), then cover and simmer for one hour.

Ten minutes before the hour is up, heat the milk and cream together in a small pot. The mixture should be hot, but do not let it boil.

Stir the milk and cream into the soup. Serve immediately.

Yield: 5 servings.

*The kind of beer you include is strictly a matter of personal taste—or anticipation. Use Michelob for a hot date, Bud for an old girlfriend, or Heineken for a Lufthansa stewardess. Under no conditions do you use light beer; if it doesn't get Rodney Dangerfield any respect, what's it going to do for you?

U.S.D.A. Government Regulation Popovers

If you're going to make a decent popover, you've got to follow the rules. This should be no problem for a Real Man, since he's been playing according to Hoyle, drawing the line, doing it by the book and laying down the law his whole life.

(Yes, we admit it's true that some rules are made to be broken, but not the ones you end up eating.)

THE RULES:

1. Milk and eggs must be at room temperature.
2. The eggs must be thoroughly beaten.
3. The muffin tins and oven must be hot.
4. Do not open the oven door while the popovers are cooking.

INGREDIENTS

> 4 *eggs*
> 2 *cups flour*
> 2 *cups milk*
> 2 *tablespoons melted butter*
> ½ *teaspoon salt*
> *muffin tins*
> *butter to grease the tins*

First, place the muffin tins in your oven and preheat to 450 degrees.

Next, beat the eggs in a large bowl, then add the flour, milk, melted butter, and salt, mixing until well blended.

Once the oven and tins are hot, butter the tins (using a stick of butter like a pencil), fill each tin two-thirds of the way up with batter and immediately place each tin in the oven.

Bake at 450 degrees for 20 minutes. Turn the oven down to 350 degrees for another 20 minutes.

Remove and serve.

Yield: 2 dozen

Beef Bourguignon

We admit it.

Bourguignon is a *French* name.

And while we generally have no use for the country that taught the world bad manners and how to surrender, this recipe was simply too delicious to leave out.

So if you're cooking for your buddies, just tell them Beef Bourguignon plays goalie for the Montreal Canadiens—and it's named after his grandfather, who invented the puck.

But if you're cooking for a woman, don't worry.

One taste and she'll think you're James Bond.

INGREDIENTS

- 12 *ounces bacon*
- 6 *pounds stewing beef*
- 2 *sliced carrots*
- 2 *sliced onions*
  salt and pepper
- 4 *tablespoons flour*
- 6 *cups red wine*
- 2 *tomatoes, chopped*
- 6 *cups canned beef bouillon*
- 2 *bay leaves*
- 1 *teaspoon thyme*
- 4 *cloves of garlic, mashed*
  cooking oil

Take the bacon, place it in a pot of water and simmer it over a low flame for 10 minutes. Then remove the bacon and cut it into small pieces.

Place three tablespoons of oil in a skillet and sauté the bacon until brown. Remove the bacon, leaving the fat in the skillet.

Next, cut the beef into 2-inch cubes, then brown the cubes on all sides in the oil that remains in the skillet. Add more oil when necessary.

Set the beef aside and brown the carrots and onions in the fat.

Place the bacon, beef and vegetables in a large casserole; season with salt and pepper to taste. Sprinkle on the flour and toss the ingredients.

Place the casserole in a 400-degree oven until the flour browns. (Toss several times to make sure the flour is cooked; this entire process should take 10 minutes.)

Add the remaining ingredients to the casserole and cover.

Turn the oven down to 325 degrees and cook for three to four hours, or until the beef is fork tender. Remove the beef and boil the liquid away until half is left.

Reheat beef in sauce.

Yield: 4–6 servings

Stuffed Mother-in-Law Chicken

Alas, every once in a while you're forced to break bread with the biggest bread breaker in your life.

This is a dish that will help you survive this ordeal.

It will not only lead your mother-in-law to believe that you actually spend time in the kitchen, but it'll also keep her so busy eating that she won't have time to complain about the money you spent on the 280Z, your excessive drinking habits or the fact that you haven't taken her daughter on a decent vacation in three years.

We'd all like to stuff our mothers-in-law.

This is the only way to do it legally.

STUFFING INGREDIENTS
- 6 *cups of crustless day-old bread, cut into half-inch cubes*
- ½ *cup minced parsley*
- 1 *tablespoon sage*
- ½ *teaspoon thyme*
- ½ *teaspoon marjoram*
- ½ *teaspoon pepper*

Toast the bread cubes in a 275-degree oven until golden brown. Then turn the oven up to 425 degrees. Transfer the bread crumbs to a large bowl and mix in the remaining ingredients. Place aside and prepare the following:

1 *cup minced onions*
1 *minced chicken liver (from the bird you are*
stuffing)
½ *cup minced celery*
3 *tablespoons butter*

Melt the butter in a pan and sauté these ingredients for ten minutes over a medium flame. Then scrape into the stuffing mixture and beat well.

1 *egg, beaten lightly*
¼ *cup canned chicken stock*
2 *tablespoons cream*

Add these liquids to the stuffing mixture, beat until well blended and stuff into a four-pound raw roasting chicken.

Next, truss the bird. (No, this does not mean ordering some therapeutic device for it from the back of *Popular Science*. The process is also known as sealing the bird—which you can accomplish by placing aluminum foil over the open cavity and tying the legs together.)

Place the chicken in a roasting pan. Smear the chicken all over with soft butter, sprinkle it with salt and pepper—and place it on the middle shelf of a preheated 425-degree oven.

Brown the chicken for 15 minutes. Turn the oven down to 350 degrees and cook for about 90 minutes. Baste occasionally with its own juices.

To see if the chicken is done, pierce the leg joint with a fork; the juice should run clear yellow.

Yield: 4 servings

Infidelity Fricassee

Your girlfriend has just caught you in bed with her college roommate.

No matter how you slice it, your goose is cooked. You're in a jam. You're in a pickle. You're in hot water. You've gotten yourself into some fine kettle of fish— and the icing on the cake is that your girlfriend is stewing.

No, this is not the time to talk turkey.

It's the time to act like a chicken, and cook one.

Admittedly, this may seem like a half-baked idea at first.

But it's a fast way to dilute the problem before she boils over, scrambles your brains and ices the relationship.

Of course, if she fails, you might try another tack:

Tell her that if she can't stand the heat, she should get out of the bedroom.

INGREDIENTS

- 2 *pounds chicken breasts halved (bone in)*
- ½ *teaspoon salt*
- ½ *teaspoon pepper*
- 1 *cup flour*
- 1 *tablespoon butter*
- 3 *tablespoons cooking oil*
- 1 *onion, chopped*
- 2 *cups canned chicken broth*
- 1 *potato, diced*
- 1 *carrot, diced*
- ½ *pound fresh mushrooms, sliced*
  pinch of basil
- 1 *bay leaf*
- ½ *cup of cream*

Preheat oven to 350 degrees. Place the salt, pepper and flour in a large grocery bag and shake to mix the ingredients. Add the chicken breasts, and shake again until they're completely coated.

Over a medium flame, heat the butter and oil in a casserole dish, add the chicken and onion. Sauté until brown.

Add enough chicken broth to cover the meat, then add the basil and bay leaf. Cover and place in oven for 30 minutes.

After 30 minutes, add the carrot, potato and mushrooms to the dish and cook for an additional 30 minutes.

Uncover your casserole, pour in the cream, stir, serve and pray she forgives you.

Yield: 4 servings

An Important Note on Steak

In America today, there are at least 30,000 different steak recipes.

All of them are good.

Steak, you see, is the Real Man's birthday cake; and while we prefer a plain, simple sirloin, fried in a pan with a touch of butter and oil, we would not be so presumptuous as to force our will on you.

The way we see it, telling a Real Man how to prepare his steak would be like telling him how to ride his horse, drive his car or make love to his girlfriend.

And among Real Men this just isn't done.

How do you want your steak? Rare or on the hoof?

Adam's Ribs

The original Real Man recipe.

INGREDIENTS

    4 *pounds fresh pork ribs*
  1⅓ *cups canned beef consommé*
  1⅓ *cups tomato sauce*
  1⅓ *cups red wine*
  1⅓ *cups orange juice*
    4 *cloves of garlic, sliced*
    1 *teaspoon oregano*
    1 *teaspoon basil*
    4 *teaspoons salt*
   ⅔ *cup imported olive oil*

In a large roasting pan, mix all ingredients except the meat. Then add the ribs to the pan and marinate them in your refrigerator for a minimum of 24 hours.

There are two options for final preparation:

You can either bake the ribs in a 350-degree oven for 45 minutes, or just grill them on your barbecue. Either way, make sure you baste them during cooking with the marinade.

NOTE: for additional treat, try smothering the cooked ribs with the Georgia peach sauce described on page 43.

Yield: 2 servings

Ten-Penny Nail Baked Potato

Real Men nail down multibillion-dollar defense contracts.

They nail the opposing quarterback.

They nail Britt Ekland

After which, a Real Man celebrates with steak and a baked potato.

The following recipe will facilitate the cooking of the baked potato, insuring that it cooks evenly and quickly, without the outer portion drying.

After all, it's the Real Man who should be hard as nails, not his baked potato.

INGREDIENTS

> *Idaho baking potatoes*
> *ten-penny nails*
> *a hammer*

Scrub your spuds and drain them.

One at a time, stand the potatoes up on end and drive a nail through the center, lengthwise.

Bake in a 375-degree oven until soft when pierced with a fork.

Add sour cream, chives, crumbled bacon, shredded cheese or sautéed garlic with melted butter to taste.

TECHNICAL NOTE: According to Mister Wizard, the nail acts as a heat conductor. He also advises that you remove it before eating.

"Going to the Mattresses" Meatballs and Spaghetti

As Clemenza told Michael Corleone:

"Hey, Mikey. Someday you might have to go to the mattresses and cook for 30 or 40 guys."

In the event you find yourself in this situation, use this recipe.

Remember: Even in the Wild West, they never killed the cook.

MEATBALL INGREDIENTS

> 4 *slices white bread*
> ¾ *cup of milk*
> 2 *pounds ground beef*
> ½ *pound sausage meat (or fresh ground pork)*
> ½ *cup grated Parmesan cheese*
> 4 *tablespoons chopped parsley*
> 2 *tablespoons chopped garlic*
> ½ *teaspoon allspice*
> 2 *teaspoons grated lemon peel*
> 2 *teaspoons salt*
> 2 *eggs beaten*

Tear up the bread, soak it in the milk, then squeeze the bread to remove most of the moisture.

Combine all the rest of the ingredients with the white bread. Beat the mixture until well blended. Form into golf ball-sized balls.

Place a quarter cup of oil in a skillet and heat over a high flame until smoking hot.

Brown the meatballs on all sides and remove them from the skillet.

To assemble the completed meal, place the meatballs in a large pot and cover with the pizza sauce on page 49. (You'll have to increase the recipe five times to get enough sauce to cover the meatballs.)

Cover the pot and let the meatballs simmer over a low flame for 20 minutes.

Mix with spaghetti you've boiled in a large pot with a dash of salt and two tablespoons of oil.

Yield: 30 meatballs

Seafood

Real Men love the sea.

Without the world's oceans, there would be no atomic submarines, aircraft carriers, battleships or amphibious troop carriers. And Jacques Cousteau would be a coal miner.

Real Men are also fond of lakes and rivers, because they can dredge them, dam them, shoot their rapids and cross them with suspension bridges. They also provide excellent places for hiding cars, old tires and friends who've fallen from favor.

Despite this love of aquatic acreage, however, Real Men are not particularly fond of aquatic life.

If cattle had fins, Real Men would eat more seafood.

Real Men do not eat weakfish. They don't carp on anything, flounder, clam up or cut bait. A Real Man would never eat anything called "shrimp"; he thinks tuna are better left to Russian trawlers; and let's not discuss what he thinks of crabs.

Going still further, Real Men admire barracuda, sharks, swordfish and marlin—and as such could never eat them.

Real Men think goldfish make nice house plants; they admire the name mussel, and while most Real Men view their lives as a continual struggle to swim upstream, they do not eat salmon.

Real Men *do* have one puzzling question about seafood, however.

Most seafood companies advertise fish that "doesn't have that fishy taste."

To this, Real Men wonder:

"If you don't want food that tastes fishy, why eat fish?"

Crow

Real Men do not eat crow.

Real Man
Cooking Quiz #3

Q. How many quiche-eaters does it take to have a fulfilling sexual experience?

A. Three. Two to do it, and one to talk about it on *Donahue*.

Q. What's the Real Man's idea of group therapy?

A. World War II.

I assure you, sir—'82 was an excellent year for
ketchup.

10

Desserts

A Real Man finishes what he begins.
He does not give up in the middle of a job. He does not end things in a half-assed manner. He does not run out, walk out or punt.

This same rigorous moral code can be applied to the process of finishing a dinner.

Where lesser men try to sneak dessert before the meal, a Real Man is content to wait.

Where lesser men might serve store-bought cake or ice cream, a Real Man goes the distance and creates his own.

Real Men understand that sooner or later we all get our just desserts.

And he's willing to wait, not just because it tastes better at the end of the meal—but because he realizes he needs the extra sugar to face the rest of the evening's challenges.

Smuggler's Pecan Rum Pie

You can always buy the rum for this dessert in your local liquor store; but buying it from a smuggler makes a far better story over coffee.

INGREDIENTS FOR TWO PIES

1   *cup sugar*
4   *tablespoons butter, melted*
4   *eggs, lightly beaten*
6   *tablespoons flour*
½   *cup dark rum*
½   *teaspoon salt*
2   *teaspoons almond extract*
2   *teaspoons vanilla*
2   *cups corn syrup, light or dark*

Preheat oven to 250 degrees. Beat together in a large mixing bowl, then add:

3   *cups chopped pecans*

Beat well again.

Pour the mixture into two unbaked 9-inch pie shells. (You can cheat and purchase them in the frozen-food section of your supermarket.)

Bake in a 350-degree oven for 30 to 45 minutes, or until the filling has set.

Serve hot.

Jack Daniels Cake

At last: a new way of consuming Jack Daniels.

INGREDIENTS

½   *cup unsalted butter, at room temp*
1   *cup sugar*
3   *eggs*
½   *teaspoon baking powder*
2   *generous cups flour*
½   *cup Jack Daniels*
12 *ounces currants, or raisins*
½   *pound chopped walnuts*

Preheat oven to 350 degrees. In a large bowl, beat the sugar into the softened butter until fluffy and white. Beat eggs in well.

Now, in a separate bowl, combine the baking powder and flour.

Beat the bourbon into the eggs and butter, then add the flour mixture, fruit and nuts, mixing well.

Take a loaf pan, smear it with butter and dust it with flour. Pour in the batter and bake for about one and three-quarters hours, or until a knife plunged in the center of the cake comes out dry.

Yield: 1 9x5x3 inch cake.

Beer Sherbet

Admittedly, Real Men love Baskin-Robbins' "rocky road," "German chocolate cake" and "pralines & cream."

But the company does have one shortcoming: no liquor license.

INGREDIENTS FOR ONE QUART

½ pound sugar
1 cup water
juice from half an orange
juice from half a lemon
1½ cups beer
1 egg white
5 pounds crushed ice
1 pound coarse salt

In a large saucepan, bring the water and sugar to a boil, until the bubbles appearing on the surface are thick. Let cool—then mix in the beer and fruit juices.

In a separate bowl, beat the egg white until stiff. Fold the egg white into the syrup mixture. Pour this into a three-quart saucepan.

Place the ice and salt in a stopped-up sink. Nest the saucepan in the ice and beat the mixture until the sherbet is thick.

Freeze overnight.

11

Great Moments in the Real Man Cuisine: Part Two

The setting is Havana. 1959. New Year's Eve. *The Godfather, Part II*.

When asked if he'd like a banana daiquiri, Al Pacino replies:

"No."

12

Half Time Snacks

Real Men snack.
But not because they're anxious, nervous, or upset about losing a girlfriend. (Real Men do not get nervous. And they certainly don't eat because of an anxiety attack.)

Real Men snack in order to get through half time at the Steelers game, the seventh inning stretch at a Yankees game, or the third quarter of the fiscal year.

This is not to say Real Men snack indiscriminately, however.

Real Men do not get the munchies.

Real Men do not nosh.

Real Men do not nibble.

And they certainly don't eat Pringles, Bon-Bons, California dip, tea biscuits, finger sandwiches, fruit, anything stuffed in an olive, or any substance that contains more than .0001 percent of the U.S.D.A. minimum daily vitamin requirement.

Granted, you may say the following recipes are nutritionally bankrupt.

But they *do* taste good.

It started as a friendly disagreement over hockey players, but then they started comparing chili recipes, and things got nasty.

New York City Street Vendor Pretzels

The kind you love to eat, but are usually afraid to touch.

(Even Real Men worry about who's been touching their food.)

To start, take a large bowl and dissolve one package of active dry yeast in cup of lukewarm water. Then add:

1½ cups flour
2 tablespoons vegetable shortening
2 tablespoons salt
1 tablespoon sugar

Beat his mixture thoroughly for at least three minutes. Then add:

1¼ cups flour

Now, knead the dough until it is no longer sticky. Place it in a bowl smeared with butter and let it sit in a draft-free area until the dough has doubled in bulk.

Preheat the oven to 475 degrees. Punch the dough down and divide it into 12 pieces. Roll the pieces into 18-inch lengths and form them into pretzel shapes.

(In case you're not familiar with this form, try to imagine the intersection of Routes 1, 9, 22 and 278, McCarter Highway and the New Jersey Turnpike outside Newark Airport. If this is too mind-boggling to imagine, just feel sorry for the people who have to drive it every day—and buy a can of Pabst, which features a pretzel-shaped logo.)

Once you've formed the pretzels, bring four quarts of water and five tablespoons of baking soda to a rolling boil.

Carefully lower each pretzel into the water and boil for one minute, or until it floats to the surface.

Transfer the pretzels to a greased baking sheet and sprinkle them with coarse salt.

Bake for 12 minutes, or until they're golden brown.

Charge at least $1 apiece.

Oreo Centers

The Oreo is as basic to the fabric of American culture as Coca-Cola, the Marlboro Man, a Chevy Impala, or speeding tickets. They're the standard bill o' fare at Boy Scout Eagle ceremonies, Red Cross blood drives, and virtually every hurricane relief center.

But while there is great discussion among Real Men over the virtues of double-stuffed Oreos *versus* the purist's standard cookie, there's one thing everyone agrees on:

The only way to eat this fabled delicacy is to split it in half and eat the center first.

(The psychological reasons for this are many and varied; some liken it to the opening of the Wild West, others, to the aphrodisiac quality of oysters. For more information on the subject, we refer you to the exhaustive research paper, "The Psycholinguistic and Socioeconomic Implications of Oreo Opening on Twentieth-Century Mankind" by Drs. Asher and Schofield, Our Mother of Perpetual Motion University, 1957. This document may still be classified. If so, we recommend suing under the Freedom of Information Act.)

With this energy-saving recipe, you'll be able to eliminate the tedious, labor-intensive process of breaking open the Oreos and just get down to eating the centers.

If all this seems confusing, just remember one thing: the French open bottles of wine; Real Men open Oreos.

INGREDIENTS
- 1½ cups confectioner's sugar
- ¼ cup water
- 1½ teaspoons vanilla
- 3 oz. vegetable shortening

In a large bowl, beat all ingredients together until mixture is firm and fluffy.

Yield: 1¼ cups

Do-It-Yourself Ring Dings

At heart, every Real Man is a handyman.

He believes he can build, fix, repair and create anything from track lighting to an F-111 without ever leaving the comfort of his basement. And no matter how many times he's gotten burned, he'd still rather try to fix the toilet himself first—and then pay the plumber twice as much to repair what he shouldn't have fooled around with in the beginning.

With this in mind, we offer a recipe that's dedicated to the do-it-yourselfer in all of us.

These Ring Dings are difficult to make and more expensive than the store-bought variety.

But after three hours, at least you'll be able to say you made them yourself.

Or make a quick run to the store and claim you did.

To start, make one recipe of chocolate sponge cake in two clean, one-pound coffee cans that you've smeared with butter and lightly floured. Place cans on baking pan. When finished, the cake should slide right out of the can; let it cool, then slice it into disks one-half inch thick.

Next, take whipped cream and make sandwiches with the disks. (The whipped cream should be about a quarter of an inch thick.)

After this is finished, dribble the chocolate icing on top, and refrigerate. When the first sides have dried, turn them over and do it again.

If you really want that store-bought feeling, you might bring in a shrinkwrapper at this point; otherwise, just sit back and feel good about not having shoplifted them.

CHOCOLATE SPONGE CAKE

> 1¼ *cups cake flour*
> 2½ *teaspoons double-acting baking powder*
> ½ *teaspoon salt*

Sift these dry ingredients together.

> 4 *ounces unsweetened chocolate*
> 1 *cup milk*
> 4 *egg yolks*
> 2 *cups confectioners' sugar*
> 1 *teaspoon vanilla*
> 4 *egg whites*

Preheat oven to 325 degrees. Melt the chocolate with the milk over a low flame. Mix well and set aside to cool.

Next, cream together the yolks, sugar and vanilla. Then beat in the chocolate mixture, followed by the dry ingredients.

Finally, fold four egg whites beaten stiff into the batter, divide batter between 2 cans, and bake for one hour and 45 minutes at 325 degrees.

WHIPPED CREAM

> 1 *cup whipping cream (cold)*
> ½ *cup confectioners' sugar*
> 1 *tablespoon vanilla extract*

Start by placing a large bowl and egg beater in the freezer for one hour. (The colder the beater and the bowl, the faster the cream will whip.)

Place the cream in the bowl and beat at high speed until the cream forms soft peaks when you remove the beater.

Add in half of the confectioners' sugar and half of the vanilla extract. Keep beating the cream (and adding the vanilla and sugar) until firm peaks appear and the cream is sweetened to your taste.

CHOCOLATE ICING

10 ounces or 2 cups semisweet chocolate
pinch of salt
1 cup sour cream

Place the semisweet chocolate in a small saucepan. Place in another pan filled with barely simmering water, and melt over a low flame.

Stir in the salt and sour cream. Blend until smooth.

Yield: 10 Ring Dings

13

Beverages

Generally speaking, Real Men do not sip, tipple, imbibe or quaff.

They drink.

They drink with friends, they drink with gusto and they occasionally guzzle.

This is not to say, however, that a Real Man will drink just anything that's been placed in front of him.

Real Men do not, for example, drink warm milk.

Real Men do not drink anything in a Polynesian glass with an umbrella sticking out of it.

Real Men do not drink anything made in a blender; they do not drink piña coladas, banana daiquiris, whiskey sours or anything that seems as if it might best be served by Don Ho on the "big island" in Hawaii.

And only in a pinch will a Real Man drink wood alcohol, Drano or turpentine.

In terms of carbonated beverages, Real Men know that Coke is the Real Thing. They do not have time for the Pepsi Challenge; a Real Man has no interest in "being a Pepper"; and if he wanted something "light and caffeine free," he'd drink water, not 7-Up.

(Needless to say, Real Men do not drink Perrier or Pelligrino; when a Real Man wants water, he gets it from a tap, not from France or Italy.)

Then there's coffee. Or joe. Or java.

To begin, Real Men do not drink "cute coffee." Coffee is a basic diet staple—and just as there's nothing cute about a Kenworth tractor trailer, an I-beam or the Hoover Dam, there's nothing cute about this serious breakfast drink. As such, Real Men do not drink cappuccino, Swiss almond, mocha, Viennese or cinnamon-flavored coffee; they won't go near anything that's been contaminated by nondairy creamer or Sweet 'N Low.* And, of course, Real Men totally reject Robert Young's admonishments about caffeine. They do not believe its elimination from your diet will improve your marriage, make you less irritable or help you get along better with the P.T.A. And Real Men *know* that cutting it out will not help you get that rig into Memphis any faster.

Of course, coffee is not the Real Man's only liquid refreshment.

Besides Jack Daniels, Real Men drink Gatorade.

They drink Tang—but only while in orbit.

And Real Men understand that while grape soda in any form is basically undrinkable, it's smart to keep a can in your car just in case you run out of Prestone.

Going still further, Real Men drink all kinds of beer. They drink dark beer, imported beer, Bud, Miller, Coors, Iron City, Pabst, Schaefer, Piels and Schlitz. And Real Men *never* drink light beer—unless somebody's paying them astronomical amounts of money to do it.

(Let's face it; with the cost of booze, beer, and broads today, Mickey Spillane must *need* the bucks, so all is forgiven.)

When it comes to social drinking, Real Men do not believe there is anything "down right upright" about a woman inviting you over for a Harvey's Bristol Cream on the rocks. If she wants to invite you over for a Bud, that's one thing; but somebody who wants to pour cream down your throat is never going to put up with fishing weekends with the boys in Colorado.

And, finally, there's the question of breakfast drinks.

---

*Among Real Men, Sweet 'N Low is considered "cute." Especially when a date orders it with cheesecake at the end of a 14-course meal.

Real Men do not drink Mimosas. It's one thing to kill a bottle of champagne at dusk on a yacht with Candice Bergen; it's quite another to kill a glass of it with orange juice at 10 o'clock in the morning.

They do not start the day with white wine spritzers, scotch and milk, or screwdrivers—despite admiring the name.

And as far as Bloody Marys are concerned, we offer the following Real Man's recipe:

The Real Man's Bloody Mary

INGREDIENTS
vodka
tomato juice
Tabasco
Worcestershire sauce
A-1 steak sauce
salt
pepper
celery

Fill a large tumbler with ice and vodka
Throw all the other ingredients away.

14

The Final Advantage to Cooking Your Own Meals

It's midnight. You and Jacqueline Bisset have just finished dinner in the most elegant part of your apartment.

The beef bourguignon was perfect. The popovers, sublime. You've displayed the table manners of Fred Astaire, using every knife, fork and spoon correctly—and not once did you get up to check the score of the Raiders game.

As you take your final sip of champagne, it's the most anxious moment of the evening.

The candles are low. The music, romantic. You look softly into her light-blue eyes; she smiles and purses her lips invitingly over the champagne glass she's brought to her mouth.

It's time for your big move.

Slowly, you reach across the table and squeeze her hand; it feels like the inside of a rose petal. You dream of satin sheets, limousine rides at dawn, and a passionate embrace at dusk on the beach at St. Martin. As your lips brush across her cheek you gently coo in her ear:

"It's your turn to take out the garbage."

Real Men, you see, understand there is no such thing as a free lunch.

Or, for that matter, a free dinner.

This looks like a good spot.